Hand Lettering 101 Workbook

Mastering Hand Lettering Workbooks Team

Table of Contents

Basics

Welcome to a fun, easy-to-use booklet on hand lettering and calligraphy! This book is a space where you can practice your hand at the art of hand lettering and calligraphy. Hand lettering and calligraphy are a little different, although they both are able to produce the same type of results. Calligraphy is the art of creating beautiful handwriting with a calligraphy pen. Hand lettering is more of a modern technique, where you are able to produce the end product of calligraphy with something other than a calligraphy pen, such as a brush, a marker, or a regular pen. For the purposes of this book, we will refer to both techniques as "hand lettering."

Hand lettering is used by many people for special occasions for their friends, relatives, or acquaintances. Some people use hand lettering in their businesses; they make printable quotes to hang on walls, or they write out wedding invitations for mass printing. Other people use hand lettering for more intimate reasons, such as writing their favorite poems in journals, creating birthday cards for close friends, or for decorating their homes. With hand lettering, the possibilities to be creative with words are endless!

Instruments

The instruments are explained in detail in each of the sections, but here is a list of what we are going to be talking about in this book:

- Premium Inkjet Paper
- Cardstock Paper
- Clairefontaine Paper
- Watercolor Paper
- Dip-Pen
- Fineliners
- Gel Pens
- Brush Pen
- Dual Brush Pen
- Water Brush
- Paint Brush
- Inkwell
- Ink
- Water Colors

Definitions:

- Baseline: The baseline is the line that the base of the letter sits on. Notice the "p" in sport. Some letters, known as "descending" letters, will go below the baseline onto the bottom line. These are letters like "p," "g," or "q." When you're doing hand lettering, the baseline is the line that each letter should "sit on."

- X-height: The x-height is the second line from the top as shown in the image above. It literally tells us the height of the letter "x." In this case, we see the height of the letters "o" and "r." Most of your lower-case letters like "a," "n," or "x" should fit in between the x-height and the baseline.

- Ascender: Ascenders are letters that extend beyond the x-height and hit the ascender height of the line, like "h," "t," or "l."

- Descender: As mentioned before, "descending" letters are letters that go below the baseline with their tails, like "p," "g," or "q." Their tails descend below the baseline and sit on the very bottom line to the descender height.

- Meanline: The meanline is the line between the baseline and the cap height, as shown in the picture above. As you can see, the meanline is the upper line of the x-height, and marks where the letters like "a" and "n" peak.

- Serif: Serif is when the letters of a typeface have feet at the bottom, like the word below:

SPORT

- Sans Serif: Sans serif literally means "without" serif. Sans serif typeface is lacking the feet at the bottom, like the word below. Notice how the word above has feet and the word below does not:

SPORT

- Downstroke: The downstroke of a letter is the part where you make a downward stroke while writing it. For example, when you write a little "c," you press downward on the left outer line to make the line thicker. The downstroke of a letter is its thickest part, and the upstroke is its thinnest part:

4

- Hairline: Hairline strokes are the upstrokes of a letter and are the thinnest part of the letter. Hairline is the opposite of a downstroke. You can see this in the "c" above. When the pen goes up, the line becomes thinner.

- Cross Stroke: The cross stroke of a letter resides in a "T" or "A," where you add a line that literally crosses through your letter. These can be straight across or wavy in order to add flare.

Now that you know some definitions, what you want to focus on while writing a word is going light on the upstroke and pressing down hard on the downstroke. This means when your writing a letter and your hand comes up, don't press hard. This will make the upstroke have a thin line. However, when you go down on a letter, press down hard. The downstroke always has a thicker line than the upstroke. This gives it that traditional calligraphy effect. At the beginning of each practice section, there will be a short section on four popular uses of hand lettering, what tools to use, and how to get started. We hope you enjoy this booklet as a fun way to learn some basic methods of hand lettering!

Exercise 1

We encourage you to go through the alphabet a couple times to get used to each letter and to develop your own style of hand lettering. Remember in this exercise: go light on the upstroke and press down hard on the downstroke, and it might be helpful to practice writing in cursive opposed to block lettering. Now, it's your turn to practice your beautiful creation! The following exercises will go a bit more in

depth, but for now, let's just stick with the basics! Write your first word: Hello.

Practice #1

Faux Calligraphy

Calligraphy is handwritten lettering that is meant to be decorative or aesthetically pleasing to the eye. We will look at "pen calligraphy" later in this booklet, which uses a pen that is meant to give the lettering that traditional calligraphy look. Faux calligraphy is a way to achieve the traditional calligraphy look without having the special pen that can form thin and wide lines with the turn of a hand. It's also a more inexpensive way to do hand lettering, because a regular pen and regular inkjet paper are sufficient here to achieve that beautiful calligraphy aesthetic.

Tools
Fineliners
Fineliners work great for faux calligraphy. Faux calligraphy is when you write a normal cursive word, then go back and create a thicker line to fill in on the downstroke. Fineliners are basically a regular pen you would write with every day; however, they are not the ball-point pens. Rather, they have long, metal tops with a fine, fiber tip.

Other Pens
Gel pens or regular ball-point pens are also appropriate tools to use when attempting faux calligraphy. Write out the word or phrase as you would in regular cursive or block letters. Then, go back over the word and fill in on the downstroke. Using gel pens would be fun if you want to make your writing colorful and shiny.

Paper
Premium inkjet paper might be the best bet to use when you're doing faux calligraphy. It's the most inexpensive paper, but it's also easy on the pen's tip. Of course, if you're wanting a sleeker, more professional-looking paper, you can always buy a hand lettering paper that is a little costlier but is made especially for calligraphy.

Method

In faux calligraphy, handwrite the lettering as you would normally with a fineline pen. The letters will have thin lines on the upstrokes as well as the downstrokes. After you write the lettering, you will go back on the downstrokes and fill in the lines to make them thicker, leaving the upstrokes alone. If you're confused about which lines to fill in, you can draw arrows on your letters to remind yourself when your hand strokes up and when your hand strokes down. For example, when you're writing a letter "n," you go up first, make a small arch, then you go down. That downstroke on the right side of the "n" is where you'll want to create a bubble and fill in that bubble. Faux calligraphy mimics real calligraphy after all is said and done. Faux calligraphy looks like the following before you fill in the downstrokes:

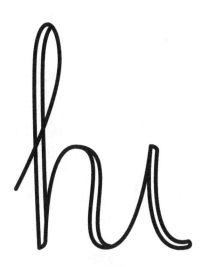

Exercise 2

For the exercises in this section, practice writing slantways. Faux calligraphy is a great way to practice writing in slant because you can make the letters very narrow with the instruments you use. Something fun to do would be to look up a favorite quote or an inspiring line of poetry. Maybe practice writing your favorite sonnet in the practice booklet. Not only will you have beautiful letters, but you will have a beautiful meaning as well! Then you can move on to writing beautiful slant cursive without the lines.

You will see that the practice lines are slanted. Just remember the basics in the last section and keep your letters within the slant, hitting appropriately in the middle of the box or at the very top line for your ascenders. Your descenders can go below the baseline. This effect will make your writing look more formal, as if you were creating a wedding invitation or a card for a baby shower.

Practice #2

Pen Calligraphy

In modern calligraphy, pen calligraphy is closest to the style of traditional calligraphy, because it is done with a pen that gives a sleek, slender look. Traditional calligraphy is slanted and has intricate embellishments; we can usually find this type of calligraphy on wedding invitations or "save the date" cards. Traditional calligraphy gives a very formal look to hand lettering.

Although traditional calligraphy is very fancy and you can try your hand at it if you want, we recommend starting with basic pen calligraphy. You can do a more informal style of pen calligraphy, an artistic style of pen calligraphy, or utilize your own unique style of pen calligraphy. This type of calligraphy is termed "Modern Calligraphy," which is just any type of calligraphy that isn't traditional calligraphy.

Tools
Dip-Pen
A dip-pen is a pen used for modern calligraphy. It has a metal, pointy tip and is usually mounted in a handle. The attraction of using a dip-pen is that you can switch out the ink to whatever you want for your desired effect: waterproof, pigmented, drawing, or acrylic ink. Dip-pens look like the following:

Ink
For pen calligraphy, you will need to buy your ink separate. Again, you can get waterproof, pigmented, drawing, or acrylic ink, depending on what look you want to achieve. You can either get an inkwell, which is a small container that holds ink inside of it, or you can pour your ink into a small cup or bowl. Dip your calligraphy pen in the bowl or inkwell and start writing!

Paper

Clairefontaine paper is an excellent paper to use if you're looking for a professional looking paper that goes well with calligraphy ink. It's a bright white color, and the ink result always looks clean. They also put out the Rhodia notepads, which are great to use for calligraphy.

Method

After you place the dip-pen in the ink, you'll dab the point of the pin on the side of the inkwell or bowl in order to get rid of the excess ink so it doesn't drip onto your paper. Then, start writing in your preferred calligraphy hand. It's helpful to press a little harder when coming down on the downstroke to achieve the traditional calligraphy look. However, don't press down too hard, or else you'll make holes in the paper.

While you're writing with the dip-pen, the ink may start getting lighter on your paper. Re-dip your ink pen as often as you want. Depending on which ink you choose, you may have to dip your pen more often to prevent the writing from getting too light. Some pens may require you to dip more, but other pens will hold the ink longer. Reading reviews on calligraphy pens and inks before you purchase them are a good way to gauge the most appropriate dip-pen and ink to buy.

Exercise 3

For the exercise in the next section, try writing a letter to someone you admire. This letter can be for someone who is living or has passed away; it can be for a public figure or a relative. Think of someone whose life you would like to model; maybe Mother Theresa? Joan of Arc? Write them and let them know what their life means to you, and how you are working to become like them every single day. The traditional calligraphy style you use in this exercise will give the letter a very formal, traditional look, so an old-school letter would be great content to pair with this style!

Practice #3

Brush Lettering

Brush lettering is hand lettering that is done with a brush pen or markers. Watercolor is also considered a type of brush lettering, but for our purposes we will wait to talk about watercolors in the next section. Brush lettering is part of modern calligraphy. The style of brush lettering is thicker than that of traditional calligraphy, which has a fine, more formal effect. Wish brush lettering you can achieve wide, bubbly letters or fat, block letters. Brush lettering is often much more forgiving in its flaws than traditional calligraphy because the fatter strokes will often hide the shakiness of your hand. Brush lettering is a great technique to learn if you want to create your own Birthday or Thank You cards, make inspiring quotes to go up in someone's home, or make any kind of writing in your home or workplace a little more fun and fancy.

Tools

Brush Pens

Brush pens are popular tools to use for hand lettering because they have the ability to trace both fine and broad lines. You can choose between a regular brush pen and a dual brush pen. Dual brush pens have a flexible brush tip and a fine brush tip all in one marker. Brush pens are water-based and thus blendable, and the nylon tip of the brush pen retains its point easily.

Markers

If you have regular markers on hand, use those for practicing! The large or small-tipped markers are great for beginners—the large-tipped may even be easier to use for hand lettering. Lightly press down on the upstroke, and then press down heavy on the downstroke in order to give your writing that calligraphy effect.

Paper

The paper you choose will depend on the type of instrument you will be using. If you are going to be using regular ink or marker, bleed-proof marker papers or cardstock paper are an excellent way to keep the ink from bleeding through the paper. Premium inkjet paper is a great paper to use if you are trying to keep expenses low, but still want paper to practice on.

Method

Similar to the other methods of hand lettering, you're going to want to press down harder on the downstroke and keep lighter on the upstroke. When you're using a regular brush pen, on the upstroke, press with the pen's tip. When you're using a brush pen on the downstroke, use more of the side of the brush and press down harder so that it will achieve a flatter look.

If you're new to lettering and only have a marker to use, that's fine too! Use the tip of the marker lightly when you're going up on the letters, and use the flat side of the marker when going down. Markers will achieve a tighter look than the brush pens, which will have more of a contrast in color.

Exercise 4

For this exercise try varying your baseline height, x-height, and ascending height for each word. This will create a more unique effect and make your lettering look like its own sort of typeface. The spontaneity of the aesthetic will be more fun for whoever is looking at your writing and will give your writing style more personality. For the content of this exercise, try writing out little signs or phrases that you think up. For example, if you built your own restaurant, what would you name it? If you could have any name in the world, what would it be? If you wrote a best-selling novel, what would its title be? Write out creative titles for all the unwritten potential in your life, and become inspired by it!

Practice #4

Water Colors

Hand lettering with water colors gives much of the same effect as brush lettering. Water color hand lettering is great for writing bubbly text or all-capitalized words or quotes. Again, creating words with water colors is easier than pen calligraphy because if you mess up on a letter or if your hand is a little shaky, it will be harder to tell, since the color is thick and more faded than the stark contrast of the pen. Let's be honest—water color brush lettering is one of our favorite mediums, especially if you use a water brush! It's just fun to be able to play with paint again!

Tools
Water-Color Disks
Water-color disks are a fun, colorful way to add flare to your hand lettering. Watercolor hand lettering is good for beginners because if you mess up on a letter or if your hand is a little shaky, the texture of the watercolor has a more rounded look and is thus more forgiving.

Water Brush or Paint Brush
Brushes are used if you want to try your hand out at water coloring. There are a couple different tools you can use for this. A "water brush" is a tool that has an empty container in the middle that you can put water in. Water brushes have nylon hairs and are stiffer than your average paint brushes. With water brushes, you squeeze the tip of it slightly so that the water comes out, dip the edge of the brush in the paint, and then start writing! Note that regular paint brushes can also be used for hand lettering. Just make sure the brush you use is narrow enough to write letters with.

Paper
Water-color paper at your local arts and crafts store is a great medium to use. Or, cardstock paper will work as well. Mostly, you'll want to stay away from regular copy paper or printer paper, because the water may soak through.

Method
For watercolor brushing, you'll want to go heavy on the downstroke and lighter on the upstroke, creating thin uplines and thick downlines. For this method, you might expect to re-dip your water or paintbrush in the paint every so often, even in the middle of some words. If the words look like they are starting to fade, you can always retrace them. Or, if you're going for a faded look, this is the perfect method to use. Your words can go from dark to faded, or from dark to faded and back to dark again. The aesthetic is totally up to you!

Let's say you're painting with the color blue and want to switch to pink. Have a spare piece of paper on the side when you watercolor. That way, when you're ready to switch colors, you can draw on the scrap piece of paper until the water brush runs clear. Then, dip your clear water brush in the pink paint and start drawing!

Note that you can write in cursive like in traditional calligraphy, or you can write in all capital letters— whatever look you are going for. Sometimes it looks cool to have a quote in all caps instead of cursive. This depends on your own style and where your drawing is going to be viewed. For all caps, you can go heavy on the downstroke, light on the upstroke, and light on the crossbars, which are the bars that go across the capital letter "A" or "T." Practice with different techniques to find out which one is your favorite.

Exercise 5

Since water brush lettering text is a little thicker, let's try writing out some of your favorite words. What word do you think of when you see your best friend? Is it "love"? What do you want for your future? Is it "Hope"? "Faith"? "Security"? What characteristics do you want to strengthen in the next few years? Is it "Courage"? "Humility"? "Inspiration"? Write down all the words that inspire you and that you seek out on a daily basis. Practicing this will make way for inspiring words and quotes all around your home!

Practice #5

CPSIA information can be obtained
at www.ICGtesting.com
Printed in the USA
LVHW062231230122
709183LV00013B/351